RECIPES & FOOD STYLING
Fiona Burrell, Janette Marshall, Jennie Shapter,
Kathryn Hawkins, Maxine Clark, Sue Ashworth

FOOD PHOTOGRAPHY
Jonathan Short, Jon Whitaker, Lighthouse Photography,
Stuart Macgregor, Upfront Photography

EDITORIAL TEAM

EDITORS
Maggie Swinburne & Stuart Johnstone

DESIGNER
Juliet Wright

PICTURES
Karen Milne, Gillian Petrie

PRODUCTION
Peter McDonald, Sarah Proctor, Babs Beaton

© DC Thomson & Co Ltd, 2021
Published in Great Britain by D C Thomson & Co. Ltd.,
185 Fleet Street, London EC4A 2HS
www.dcthomson.co.uk

62 Delicious Recipes

Spring

Fresh and easy new season
recipes for a new you

Summer

From BBQ treats to simple
salads for the warm weather

Christmas

Cosy

Refresh And Revitalise Mind, Body And Soul

We all look forward to spring for new ideas, inspiration and adventure!

Don't you just love spring? It's the season that promises new life and new hope. We cast off the gloomy, oppressive shackles of winter and look forward to the brighter days ahead.

As the days lengthen, and sunlight bathes us, animals awaken from their slumber, plants and flowers begin to bloom. The sense of renewal is palpable.

For people, spring is the time for us to enjoy all the majesty of what nature has to offer. Long walks in the sun, allowing our senses to take it all in. The sights, sounds and smells of a world reborn are very special indeed.

> *Spring is the time of plants and projects – Leo Tolstoy*

Spring is about health and inspiration, the chance to try something new – all of which you will find in these delicious, enticing and easy recipes.

Wraps

Rocket And Pear With Stilton And Pecans

Serves 2

Peel and slice 1 ripe pear and 1 fresh fig. Heat 2 flatbreads or soft flour tortillas in a chargrill pan or under the grill. Scatter a handful of rocket leaves onto each one, share the fruit between them, then crumble 40g Blue Stilton and sprinkle it on top, along with a few pecan nuts. Serve, sprinkled with black pepper.

Garlic Butter Flatbread Bites With Red Pepper Dip

Serves 2

Mix 1 crushed garlic clove with 30g softened butter and a little chopped fresh parsley. Spread over 2 flatbreads and grill for 1-2min. Mix 80g low-fat soft cheese with 80g red pepper houmous and 2tbsp chopped roasted red peppers (bottled). Cut the flatbread into triangles and serve with the dip, topped with roasted red peppers and sprinkled with chives and parsley.

RECIPES AND STYLING: SUE ASHWORTH
PHOTOGRAPHY: JONATHAN SHORT

Tomato, Avocado, Red Pepper And Onion with Golden Halloumi

Serves 2

Finely slice ½ red onion and sprinkle with a little cider vinegar. Slice a ripe avocado, quarter 4 cherry tomatoes and slice ½ red pepper (bottled or fresh). Warm 2 flatbreads or tortillas in a chargrill pan or under the grill, and top with the onion, avocado and tomatoes. Add a couple of slices of halloumi cheese, dry-fried until golden, then finish off with spoonfuls of pesto and basil leaves.

Carrot And Houmous With Poppy Seeds And Pine Nuts

Serves 2

Coarsely grate 1 medium carrot. Heat 2 wholemeal chapatis, flat breads or tortillas in a chargrill pan or under the grill. Spread each one with 2tbsp houmous. Top with the carrot and sprinkle with a few sultanas, poppy seeds and pine nuts. Crumble some feta cheese on top, and season with black pepper.

Mexican Chilli Chicken Flatbreads

Serves 2

Finely chop 1 tomato, ½ small red onion and ½ yellow pepper to make a salsa. Mash 1 ripe avocado with a squeeze of lime for the guacamole. Take 2 corn tortillas and heat them in a chargrill pan, or warm under the grill. Top with the salsa, guacamole and shreds of roast chicken breast. Finish off each one with 1tbsp soured cream, thinly sliced green chilli and chopped fresh coriander.

Grilled Peach, Parma Ham And Mozzarella

Serves 2

Heat a chargrill pan and griddle 1 sliced fresh peach or nectarine. Warm 2 flatbreads or soft flour tortillas in the chargrill pan or under the grill. Top with a few baby spinach leaves, the grilled peaches and slices of Parma ham. Add 3 mini mozzarella balls to each one, then serve, sprinkled with a little olive oil and black pepper.

Mexican Scrambled Eggs With A Lime And Coriander Salsa

Give your eggs a bit of extra zing!

Ingredients (Serves 2)

- **80g chorizo, sliced**
- **1 small red pepper, deseeded and chopped**
- **Generous handful of young spinach**
- **2 slices sourdough bread**
- **1tbsp olive oil**
- **5 eggs, beaten**
- **3tbsp milk**
- **Freshly-ground black pepper**

For the salsa

- **3tbsp chopped fresh coriander**
- **2tbsp finely chopped red onion**
- **Juice of ½ lime**
- **2tsp finely sliced red chilli**
- **Lime wedges and coriander sprigs**

1 Make the salsa by mixing together the coriander, onion, lime juice and chilli.

2 Cook the chorizo in a non-stick frying pan with the pepper for 3-4min, without oil. Add the spinach and stir until wilted.

3 Sprinkle one side of the sourdough slices with a little olive oil, then grill or chargrill until lightly browned.

4 Beat the eggs and milk together and add to the chorizo mixture. Cook, stirring, until lightly set – for 1-2min. Serve on the toast with the salsa and black pepper, garnished with lime wedges and coriander sprigs.

Enjoy this dish at any time of the day, for breakfast, lunch or dinner

RECIPE AND STYLING: SUE ASHWORTH
PHOTOGRAPHY: JONATHAN SHORT

RECIPE AND STYLING: SUE ASHWORTH
PHOTOGRAPHY: JONATHAN SHORT

Open BLT On Brioche With Avocado

A tasty snack at any time of the day

Ingredients (Serves 2)

- ◆ **4 rashers streaky bacon**
- ◆ **1 large ripe avocado, halved, pitted and peeled**
- ◆ **4 slices brioche**
- ◆ **A little butter, for spreading**
- ◆ **2 handfuls rocket**
- ◆ **3 tomatoes, sliced**
- ◆ **Freshly-ground black pepper**

1 Grill bacon until crispy. While it's cooking, mash the avocado.

2 Toast the brioche lightly. Take care – it toasts very quickly! Spread with a little butter.

3 Put the toasted brioche onto 2 serving plates. Top with rocket, sliced tomatoes, bacon and mashed avocado. Sprinkle with pepper.

COOK'S TIP:

Use granary or sourdough bread as a change from brioche

Taste Of The Med

Enjoy this healthy tapas-style feast

Ingredients (Serves 2)

- ◆ **150g thin green beans**
- ◆ **390g canned green lentils**
- ◆ **1 small yellow pepper**
- ◆ **100g Feta cheese**
- ◆ **100g sun-blush tomatoes, drained**
- ◆ **100g pitted mixed olives**
- ◆ **2tsp fresh pesto sauce**
- ◆ **Salt and freshly ground black pepper**
- ◆ **1tbsp extra virgin olive oil**
- ◆ **25g toasted pine nuts and fresh basil leaves to sprinkle**

1 Bring a saucepan of lightly salted water to the boil. Remove the stalks from the beans and cook for 4-5min until tender. Drain and rinse in cold running water to cool. Set aside.

2 Drain and rinse the lentils. Shake off excess water, then season. Halve, deseed and slice the pepper. Crumble the cheese into pieces, then arrange neatly between 2 bowls with the lentils, beans, tomatoes and olives.

3 Mix the pesto and oil together and serve alongside the bowls with pine nuts and basil leaves to sprinkle.

RECIPE AND STYLING: KATHRYN HAWKINS
PHOTOGRAPHY: STUART MACGREGOR

17

Indian Express

A fresh, zesty and colourful bowlful

Ingredients (Serves 2)

- **Salt**
- **100g Basmati rice**
- **½ prepared ripe mango**
- **200g skinless cooked chicken**
- **8 cherry tomatoes**
- **100g cucumber**
- **1 small red onion**
- **100g coconut yogurt**
- **2tbsp mango chutney**
- **Fresh mint to sprinkle**

1 Bring a saucepan of lightly salted water to the boil. Rinse the rice, then cook for 10-12min until tender. Drain and rinse under cold running water to cool. Drain well and set aside.

2 Slice the mango and chicken. Quarter the tomatoes, and slice the cucumber. Peel and thinly slice the onion. Arrange the rice, chicken, mango and vegetables neatly between 2 bowls.

3 Lightly marble the yogurt and chutney together and serve with the bowls, with fresh mint leaves to sprinkle.

Broad Bean Feta Mint Salad

Versatile and bursting with flavour

Ingredients (Serves 2)

- **80g mixed grains**
- **200g broad beans, fresh or frozen**
- **Juice of 1 orange**
- **1tbsp olive oil**
- **4 large mint leaves, finely chopped**
- **100g feta crumbled**
- **200g mixed leaves**

1 Boil or soak the grains as instructed, usually around 12-15min. Drain and rinse if necessary.

2 Boil the beans for about 10min or as instructed on the pack for frozen.

3 Mix the orange juice and olive oil. Season and stir in the mint leaves. Toss the grains and beans in the dressing and tip onto a bed of salad leaves. Crumble the feta over the top and serve.

RECIPE AND STYLING: JANETTE MARSHALL
PHOTOGRAPHY: JON WHITAKER

Prawn Laksa

Wake up your tastebuds!

Ingredients (Serves 2)

- 80g laksa paste
- 250ml reduced fat coconut milk
- 500ml fish or chicken stock
- 200g large, peeled uncooked prawns, thawed if frozen
- 100g fresh bean sprouts
- 100g dry rice stick noodles
- 80g cucumber, cut into thin strips
- 2 radish, cut into thin strips
- A small bunch fresh coriander, chopped
- A little chopped red chilli

1 Put the paste in a large saucepan and blend in the coconut milk and stock. Bring to the boil and simmer for 2min. Stir in the prawns and simmer gently for about 5min until the prawns are pink and cooked through. Stir in the beansprouts, cover and stand for 5min.

2 Meanwhile, put the noodles in a heatproof bowl. Cover with boiling water and leave to soften for 5min, then drain and divide between 2 warm bowls.

3 To serve, ladle over the prawn broth. Mix the remaining ingredients together and pile on top. Serve immediately.

Fish Pie Pancakes

Try this new take on the humble fish pie

Ingredients (Serves 2)

- **110g plain flour**
- **Pinch salt**
- **1 large egg**
- **250ml milk**
- **A few drops of vegetable oil**

Filling

- **300g pack fish pie mix (salmon, cod and smoked haddock)**
- **300ml milk**
- **25g plain flour**
- **25g butter**
- **2tbsp chopped fresh parsley, plus sprigs to garnish**
- **Salt and freshly ground black pepper**
- **Lemon wedges, to serve**

Try other tasty fillings by swapping the fish for chicken or mushrooms

1 Preheat the oven to 180°C, Fan Oven 160°C, Gas Mark 4. Put the flour and salt into a mixing bowl and add the eggs and milk. Beat together using a hand whisk to make a smooth batter. Allow to stand for a few minutes.

2 Heat a heavy-based pancake pan, and add a few drops of vegetable oil. Pour in one quarter of the batter, tilting the pan to spread over the surface. Cook over a medium heat, and when set, flip over to cook the other side. Cool on sheets of kitchen paper. Make 4 pancakes, adding a little vegetable oil to the pan each time.

3 For the filling, put the fish pie mix into a pan and cover with water. Simmer gently for 5min. Remove from the heat.

4 Put the milk, flour and butter into a non-stick saucepan and bring to the boil, stirring constantly with a small whisk until thickened and smooth. Add the cooked fish, using a draining spoon, then add the parsley. Season. Thin the sauce with a little fish cooking liquid if necessary.

5 Fill the pancakes with the fish mixture and fold into triangles or roll them up. Place in a baking dish and cover with foil. Bake for 20-25min until heated through. Serve, garnished with parsley and lemon wedges.

RECIPE AND STYLING: JANETTE MARSHALL
PHOTOGRAPHY: JON WHITAKER

Salmon Tagliatelle

This dish is spring in a bowl!

Ingredients (Serves 2)

- ◆ **2 x 110g salmon fillets**
- ◆ **150g tagliatelle**
- ◆ **150g fresh or frozen peas**
- ◆ **1tbsp chopped fresh parsley**
- ◆ **100ml half fat crème fraiche**
- ◆ **Juice of 1/2 lemon**

1 Poach the salmon pieces for about 15min in a covered pan with enough water to come half way up the fish. Drain and flake the fish

2 Boil the pasta for about 12min until al dente, adding the peas for the final 5-6min.

3 Drain the pasta and return to the warm pan to stir in the crème fraiche, lemon juice and parsley. Season and stir in the flaked salmon.

Use different fish for a change

Chicken And Avocado Fajitas

Colourful and spicy!

Ingredients (Serves 2)

- ◆ **200g skinless chicken**
- ◆ **1tsp dukka spice mix**
- ◆ **1 onion**
- ◆ **1 garlic clove**
- ◆ **75g natural yogurt**
- ◆ **1 red pepper**
- ◆ **1tbsp rapeseed oil**
- ◆ **1 avocado**
- ◆ **1 lime**
- ◆ **1tbsp chopped fresh parsley**
- ◆ **2 tortilla**

1 Cut the chicken into strips or chunks. Dice the onion and garlic and mix into the yogurt with the spice. Marinate the chicken in the fridge for 1hr.

2 Halve the peppers, deseed and grill, skin side up, or hold over a gas flame until the skin is blistered. When cooled peel off the skin and slice.

3 Griddle the marinated chicken over a hot heat for about 10min or until cooked.

4 Peel and stone the avocados and chop roughly into a bowl with the juice of one lime. Season and stir in the parsley.

5 Arrange the ingredients on the fajita and garnish with wedges of the remaining lime.

Crispy Beef And Rice Noodles

Rich and delicious!

Ingredients (Serves 2)

- **200g beef mince**
- **1tbsp vegetable oil**
- **4 spring onions, chopped**
- **2 garlic cloves, crushed**
- **300g cooked thin rice noodles**
- **1tbsp dark soy sauce**
- **1tbsp sweet chilli sauce**
- **¼ Chinese leaves, shredded**
- **Small bunch fresh coriander, roughly chopped**
- **A few fresh mint leaves, roughly chopped**
- **Lime wedges and chopped red chilli to serve**

1 Heat a wok or large frying pan until hot; add 1tbsp oil and stir fry the beef over a high heat for about 5min until brown and crispy. Drain, reserving juices and keep warm.

2 Reheat pan juices, and stir fry spring onions and garlic for 1min. Add the noodles, soy sauce and sweet chilli sauce, then stir fry for a further 2-3min until thoroughly hot. Turn off the heat, stir in the Chinese leaves, cover and stand for 5min to wilt the leaves.

3 Stir in the chopped herbs and crispy beef and pile into warm serving bowls. Serve with fresh lime and red chilli.

Easy Mango "Cheesecake"

A simple but indulgently creamy dessert

Ingredients (Serves 2)

- ◆ **1 very ripe small mango**
- ◆ **75ml half fat cream cheese**
- ◆ **1tsp caster sugar**
- ◆ **Juice of half a lime**
- ◆ **1tbsp half fat crème fraiche**
- ◆ **2 reduced fat digestive biscuits**
- ◆ **1 ripe small passion fruit**

1 Peel mango and cut fruit away from the stone. Put in a food processor and process until smooth. Add cream cheese, sugar, lime juice and crème fraiche and process until well mixed. Add a little extra lime juice or sugar as required. Pour into a bowl and refrigerate for 2hrs.

2 To assemble, crush the biscuits in a plastic bag until they are broken into small pieces but still have some texture. Layer up the cheesecakes just before serving as follows: put a layer of biscuits into the bottom of 2 glasses, then carefully pour half the mango mixture on top. Scatter the remaining biscuits over the top and finish with the last of the mango.

3 Cut the passion fruit in half and spoon the seeds on top of each pudding. Serve immediately to avoid the biscuits going soggy.

You can use different fruits to create different flavours

RECIPE AND STYLING: FIONA BURRELL
PHOTOGRAPHY: LIGHTHOUSE

Blueberry, Pecan And Mini Egg Muffins

A sweet treat for Easter – or at any time!

Ingredients (Makes 12)

- **80g rolled oats**
- **200g plain flour**
- **Pinch of salt**
- **1tsp bicarbonate of soda**
- **1½tsp baking powder**
- **125g light muscovado sugar**
- **1 large egg, beaten**
- **1tsp vanilla extract**
- **120ml milk**
- **200g low-fat plain yogurt**
- **80g butter, melted**
- **100g blueberries**
- **50g pecan nuts, chopped**
- **12 mini chocolate eggs, halved**

For the topping

- **200g ricotta cheese**
- **½tsp vanilla extract**
- **2tbsp icing sugar**
- **Blueberries, pecan nuts and mini chocolate eggs**

1 Preheat oven to 190°C, Fan Oven 170°C, Gas Mark 5. Put 12 paper cases into a muffin tin.

2 Put the oats, flour, salt, bicarbonate of soda and baking powder into a large bowl and stir in the sugar.

3 In a separate bowl, beat together egg, vanilla, milk, yogurt and melted butter. Tip into dry ingredients and add blueberries, pecan nuts and mini eggs, stirring until just combined. Do not beat. Share between muffin cases. Bake for 22-25min until risen and golden. Cool on a wire rack.

4 Mix ricotta, vanilla and icing sugar together. Spoon onto the muffins and decorate with blueberries, pecan nuts and mini eggs.

Experiment with different flavourings and toppings

Raspberry Frangipane Slices

An elegant classic that everyone will love

Ingredients

- **500g ready-made, all-butter shortcrust pastry**
- **115g butter, softened**
- **115g caster sugar**
- **2 eggs**
- **2tbsp double cream**
- **115g ground almonds**
- **2tbsp flour**
- **150g fresh raspberries**
- **Icing sugar**

1 Preheat the oven to 200°C, Fan Oven 180°C, Gas Mark 6. Place a baking sheet in the oven to heat. Roll out the pastry and line a 17 x 28cm oblong flan tin with it. Prick the base and chill until the filling is ready.

2 Cream the butter and add the sugar. Beat until light and soft. Beat the egg and beat into the mixture a little at a time. Add the double cream. Stir in the almonds and flour.

3 Spread the filling into the pastry case and lay the raspberries on top, pressing them down gently.

4 Bake in the oven on the hot baking sheet for 15min until the top is beginning to brown. Turn the oven down to 180°C, Fan Oven 160°C, Gas Mark 4 and cook for a further 15-20min or until the frangipane is cooked.

5 Remove from the oven and allow to cool in the tin. Just before serving, dust with icing sugar. Serve warm or cold.

Enjoy with a cuppa for afternoon tea, or with custard for pudding

Sit Back And Let The Summer Sizzle!

Life is busy, time is precious, but summer is your moment to slow down and relax

Things are hotting up! Long days of blue skies and the warm glow of summer bathing our skin – it's perfection. Summer is a time of both adventure and relaxation. All that matters is feeling the heat of the sun on our skin.

Light, summer dresses, shorts and T-shirts – this is the time of year to dress down to dress up! It doesn't matter if you are taking long walks in the pleasant evening haze, or enjoying a ice-cold drink with friends in your garden, this season is all about leisure – to relax and enjoy yourself with the people who matter to you most.

During summer our food is bright and colourful, packed with

> **Smell the sea and see the sky. Let your soul and spirit fly – Van Morrison**

goodness and tasting amazing. These wonderful recipes are all you need to enjoy your very own sunshine spectacular meals and treats.

Sticky Pork Ribs

Get the seal of approval from your family
and friends with this finger-licking recipe
for juicy marinated ribs

Ingredients

- 1 small red onion
- 2tbsp olive oil
- 1 red or
  green chilli
- 1 garlic clove

- 3tbsp tomato
  purée
- 1tsp salt
- Freshly ground
  black pepper

- 1 lime or lemon
- 2tbsp soy sauce
- 4tbsp clear honey
- 1kg pork ribs

1 Gather the marinade ingredients. Most marinade mixtures are made of a combination of tomato purée or ketchup, soy sauce, hoisin sauce or oyster sauce, honey, citrus juice and spices – though you can add chilli sauce, garlic, ginger, flavoured oils, vinegar and herbs. Have a large bowl ready (not metal) for combining the marinade with the ribs.

2 Peel the red onion and chop it very finely. Heat the olive oil in a non-stick frying pan. Add the onion and fry very gently over a low heat for 5-6min, stirring often. Another time, you could use a small regular onion, 4 shallots or 4-6 trimmed and finely chopped spring onions instead. Just cook until softened, but not browned. Add a splash of water, if necessary.

RECIPE AND STYLING: SUE ASHWORTH
PHOTOGRAPHY: JONATHAN SHORT

> " Allow plenty
> of time for
> marinating to
> achieve the
> best flavour –
> overnight is best!

3 While the onion is cooking, split the chilli lengthways with a small, sharp knife and scrape out the seeds. Chop it very finely. Peel the clove of garlic, then crush it with the back of cook's knife, or use a garlic crusher. If you love garlic, feel free to add an extra clove. Tip the chilli and garlic into the frying pan, stir well and cook gently for 3-4min.

4 Using a cook's measuring spoon for accuracy, add 3tbsp tomato purée to the pan and stir in. Add 150ml cold water, stir until just mixed, then remove from the heat. Transfer marinade to the large bowl. Season with 1tsp salt and plenty of freshly-ground black pepper. You could use tomato ketchup instead of purée, but the flavour will be sweeter.

5 Finely grate the zest from the lime or lemon, then squeeze the juice. Add this to the bowl with the soy sauce and honey. Stir well, or use a small whisk to mix all the ingredients together. If you like, you could prepare this marinade ahead of time, and keep it in a screw-topped jar in the fridge for 3-4 days before you plan to use it.

6 Add the pork ribs to the bowl, using your hands to turn them in the marinade, until they are all coated. Cover with cling film, then refrigerate for several hours – overnight is even better. If you remember, it's a good idea to toss the ribs in the marinade once or twice to ensure all the ribs absorb the flavours of the ingredients.

TIP: If you want to make washing-up easier, line the roasting tin with foil first!

7 When ready to cook, preheat oven to 200°C/fan oven 180°C/Gas Mark 6. Tip ribs into a large roasting tin, reserving the marinade. Roast for 55-60min, basting with the marinade after the first 20min, then again after 40min. At this point, tip any remaining marinade over the ribs.

Added Extras

Asian Veg Coleslaw

Enjoy hints of Far Eastern flavours in this fresh, crunchy coleslaw. Finely slice 1 red and 1 yellow pepper, combine with 1 grated carrot, 6 thinly sliced radish, 2 sliced celery sticks and half a finely shredded sweetheart cabbage. Mix 2tbsp each sweet chilli sauce, sesame oil and lime juice and toss through the coleslaw.

Sweetcorn With Baste

Halve 4 corn cobs and boil in lightly salted water for 10min. Meanwhile, mix 2tbsp honey with the juice of 1 small orange and 20g melted butter. Drain the corn cobs and cook in a char-grill pan or frying pan for 4-5min (or over barbecue coals), brushing with the baste and turning often.

Mango And Cucumber Salsa

Finely chop 1 ripe mango, 1 very small red onion and a cucumber portion. Season with a little vinegar, lemon or lime juice, salt and pepper and a pinch of sugar. Chop a little parsley or coriander on top, and serve as a side dish.

RECIPE AND STYLING: SUE ASHWORTH
PHOTOGRAPHY: JONATHAN SHORT

French Toast With Poached Apricots And Strawberries

Where has this dish been all your life?

Ingredients (Serves 2)

- **3 apricots, pitted and quartered**
- **2tbsp light muscovado sugar**
- **100g strawberries, halved**
- **2 thick slices sourdough bread, cut in half diagonally**
- **1 egg**
- **150ml milk**
- **1tsp vanilla extract**
- **25g butter**
- **Icing sugar, for sprinkling**
- **Greek-style yogurt or crème fraiche, to serve**
- **Mint leaves, to decorate**

1 Put the apricots into a saucepan with 100ml water and the muscovado sugar. Simmer for 5-6min, or until just tender. Remove from the heat and add the strawberries.

2 In a large shallow bowl, beat together the egg, milk and vanilla extract. Add bread and leave to soak, turning once.

3 Melt the butter in a large pan. Fry the soaked bread for 1-2min until set and golden brown. Turn and cook the other side for a further 1-2min.

4 Share between two bowls. Top with the warm fruit, then garnish with icing sugar and mint. Serve with Greek yogurt.

Perfect for an indulgent breakfast or leisurely weekend brunch

45

Mushroom And Roasted Pepper Omelette

Three steps to lunch heaven. Just try it!

Ingredients (Serves 2)
- 2 eggs
- 2tbsp milk
- 2tsp vegetable oil
- 80g mushrooms, sliced
- 80g roasted red pepper (from a jar), chopped
- Salt and freshly ground black pepper
- Salad leaves and fresh herbs, to garnish

1 Beat the eggs and milk together well and set aside for now.

2 Heat the vegetable oil in a non-stick frying pan and fry the mushrooms for 3-4min, until browned. Add the pepper and stir together.

3 Pour the egg mixture into the pan and cook for 1-2min to make an omelette. Season, then serve, garnished with salad leaves and fresh herbs.

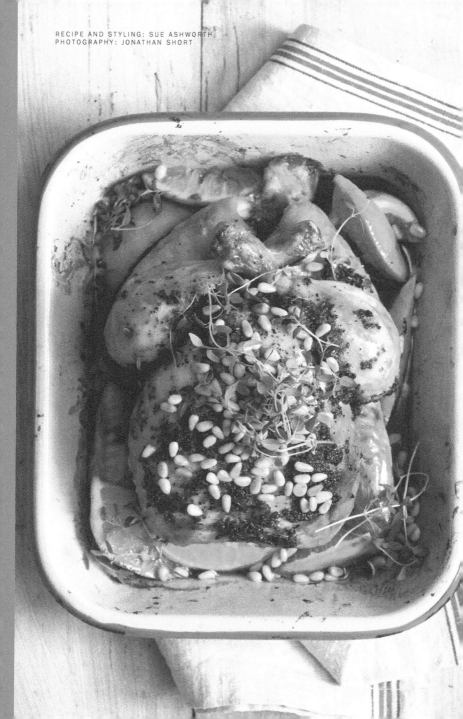

Roast Chicken With Orange, Thyme And Pine Nuts

Take a simple roast to another level

Ingredients
(Serves 2, with leftovers)

- **1 medium chicken**
- **1 small orange**
- **20g butter, softened**
- **1tbsp chopped fresh thyme (or 1tsp dried thyme)**
- **1tbsp wholegrain mustard**
- **20g pine nuts**
- **Salt and freshly ground black pepper**
- **Thyme sprigs, to garnish**

1. Preheat the oven to 200°C, fan oven 180°C, Gas Mark 6. Put the chicken into a roasting tin.

2. Finely grate the zest from the orange, then cut the orange into wedges. Mix the zest with the butter, chopped thyme or dried thyme and mustard. Rub all over the chicken. Season with salt and black pepper.

3. Cover the bird with foil and roast for 1hr. Remove the foil and baste the chicken, then add the orange wedges. After a further 15min, sprinkle the pine nuts on top.

4. Roast for 1hr 30min-1hr 40min in total. Check that the chicken is fully cooked by inserting a sharp knife into the thickest part. There should be no trace of pink juices. If necessary, cook for a little longer.

5. Cover the chicken with foil and allow it to rest for 10min before carving. Serve, garnished with thyme sprigs.

Serve with baby roast potatoes and steamed leeks, or a salad of crisp leaves

Chicken And Chickpea Tortilla Bowl

A joyful mix of colour and flavour

Ingredients (Serves 2)

- **2 soft flour tortillas**
- **A little vegetable oil**
- **2-3 iceberg lettuce leaves, shredded**
- **1tbsp olive oil**
- **1tbsp lemon juice**
- **1tsp Dijon mustard**
- **400g can chickpeas, rinsed and drained**
- **1 medium carrot, grated**
- **20g raisins or sultanas**
- **1tsp black onion seeds (optional)**
- **100g roast chicken, chopped**
- **6 cherry tomatoes**
- **Salt and freshly ground black pepper**

1 Preheat the oven to 200°C, fan oven 180°C, Gas Mark 6.

2 Brush the tortillas with a little vegetable oil, then fit them into two ovenproof basins, such as pudding bowls. Bake for 5-6min, until lightly browned. Cool for a few moments, then transfer to serving plates and add a small amount of lettuce to each one.

3 In a large bowl, mix together the olive oil, lemon juice and mustard. Then add the chickpeas, half the grated carrot, raisins or sultanas, black onion seeds (if using) and chicken. Season.
Share between the tortilla bowls. Serve with the cherry tomatoes and the reserved grated carrot.

The chickpeas add protein and fibre, making this simple dish more filling and nutritious

RECIPE AND STYLING: SUE ASHWORTH
PHOTOGRAPHY: JONATHAN SHORT

Citrus Chicken, Avocado And Warm Quinoa Salad

Simple superfoods!

Ingredients (Serves 2)

- ◆ **250g pack microwaveable quinoa**
- ◆ **1 red or pink grapefruit**
- ◆ **1 ripe avocado, halved, pitted, peeled and sliced**
- ◆ **200g roast chicken, torn into shreds**
- ◆ **Salt and freshly ground black pepper**
- ◆ **2 handfuls young spinach leaves or mixed leaves**
- ◆ **Olive oil, for drizzling**

1. Prepare the quinoa in the microwave following the pack instructions.

2. Remove all the peel and pith from the grapefruit using a sharp, serrated knife. Cut into segments, removing all the pith. Mix gently with the avocado, warm quinoa and chicken. Season.

3. Share between 2 plates with the spinach leaves or mixed leaves. Serve, drizzled with a little olive oil.

Creamy Spinach And Broccoli Soup

A refreshing soup to put a spring in your step

Ingredients (Serves 2)

- **6 spring onions, chopped (or use 1 small onion)**
- **200g broccoli, broken into florets**
- **800ml vegetable stock**
- **150g spinach, thoroughly washed**
- **100g low fat soft cheese**
- **1-2tbsp milk**
- **Salt and freshly ground black pepper**

1 Put the spring onions, broccoli and stock into a large saucepan. Bring to the boil, then reduce the heat and simmer, partially covered, for 10-15min.

2 Reserve a few spinach leaves for garnish. Add the rest to the saucepan and stir them in – they will wilt down.

3 Transfer the soup to a blender or food processor. Reserve 2tbsp soft cheese. Add the rest to the blender and blend until smooth. (Alternatively, use a hand-held stick blender to purée the soup).

4 Re-heat the soup and season to taste. Mix the reserved soft cheese with the milk. Serve it spooned on to the soup, garnished with spinach leaves.

Wilt then blend the spinach quickly to keep the fresh colour

Roast Cod with Mushroom And Tomato Salsa

A flavoursome meal fresh from the Med

Ingredients (Serves 1)

- ◆ **2tbsp olive oil**
- ◆ **1 very small onion or 3 spring onions, finely chopped**
- ◆ **80g mushrooms, finely chopped**
- ◆ **1 large tomato, finely chopped**
- ◆ **2tsp tomato purée**
- ◆ **1 slice sourdough bread**
- ◆ **1 fillet frozen cod loin, thawed (or use fresh)**
- ◆ **Salt and freshly ground black pepper**
- ◆ **Parsley sprigs, chopped dill and lemon wedges, to garnish (optional)**

1 Preheat the oven to 190°C, Fan 170°C, Gas Mark 5.

2 Heat 1tbsp olive oil in a frying pan. Add the onion and mushrooms and fry gently for 6-8min, until very soft. Add the tomato and cook for 1-2min. Stir in the tomato purée. Season.

3 Put the bread into a small roasting tin and sprinkle with a few drops of olive oil. Spread thickly with the vegetable mixture. Place the fish fillet on top and drizzle with the remaining oil.

4 Bake for 12-15min, until the fish is opaque and flakes easily. Serve, garnished with herb sprigs and lemon wedges.

If using defrosted fish, blot with kitchen paper to remove as much water as possible before roasting

Easy Prawn Biriyani

Medium spiced, yet deliciously light

Ingredients (Serves 2)
- 175g long grain rice
- 2tbsp vegetable oil
- 4 spring onions, finely chopped
- 2tsp medium curry powder
- ½tsp cumin seeds
- 100g roasted red pepper (from a jar), chopped
- 75g frozen peas, thawed
- 150g frozen prawns, thawed
- Salt and freshly ground black pepper
- 4tbsp Greek-style natural yogurt
- 20g cucumber, finely chopped

Serve with mini naan, or poppadoms for extra crunch

1 Cook the rice in lightly salted boiling water for 10-12min, until tender.

2 Meanwhile, heat oil in a large pan and gently fry the spring onions for 3-4min, until softened. Add the curry powder and cumin seeds and stir for 1min, then add the roasted pepper, peas and prawns. Cook, stirring, for 2-3min.

3 Drain the rice and add it to the pan. Season and stir well. Serve with the yogurt mixed with the cucumber.

Indian-Style Meat And Two Veg

Why not spice up the traditional burger?

Ingredients (Serves 2)

- **250g lean minced beef**
- **15g onion, finely chopped**
- **1 clove garlic, crushed**
- **25g mild curry paste**
- **50g cooked peas, mashed**
- **50g cooked potato, finely chopped**
- **½tsp salt**
- **1 medium egg, beaten**
- **1tsp vegetable oil**
- **4 mini naan, toasted**
- **Sliced red onion, tomato, cucumber and coriander, to serve**
- **2tbsp mango chutney**

1 Put the mince in a bowl and mix in the onion, garlic, curry paste, peas, potato and salt. Bind together with the egg. Divide into 2 equal portions and form each into a burger shape about 10cm diameter. Put on a plate lined with baking parchment, cover and chill for 30min or until ready to cook.

2 When ready to serve, brush a non-stick frying pan lightly with oil and heat until hot. Add the burgers, reduce to a medium heat and cook for 8-10min on each side until cooked through.

3 Top 2 naans with onion, tomato and cucumber and a burger. Spoon over the mango chutney and add coriander. Sandwich together with another naan and serve immediately.

If you prefer, finely chop the tomato, cucumber and red onion to make an Indian kachumber salad

A Proper Veggie Burger

Ingredients (Serves 2)

- **2 large Portobello mushrooms**
- **20g toasted pine nuts**
- **50g cooked mushroom rice**
- **25g freshly grated Parmesan cheese**
- **20g garlic butter**
- **2 Mozzarella cheese slices**
- **2 large wholegrain rolls, split and toasted**
- **½ ripe medium avocado, sliced**
- **A handful of watercress**

1 Preheat the oven to 200°C, Fan Oven 180°C, Gas Mark 6. Wipe the mushrooms. Remove and chop the stalks. Mix the stalks with the pine nuts, rice and Parmesan and spoon into the mushrooms. Sit the mushrooms side by side a shallow baking dish. Dot with garlic butter.

2 Pour 10ml boiling water into the dish, cover with foil and bake for 10min. Uncover and cook for a further 15min until tender and lightly golden.

3 To serve, drain the mushrooms and place in the rolls. Top with sliced cheese, avocado and watercress. Pop the lid on and serve immediately.

RECIPE AND STYLING: KATHRYN HAWKINS
PHOTOGRAPHY: LIGHTHOUSE PHOTOGRAPHY

Hawaiian Turkey And Bacon Burger

Aloha! Simply sunshine in a bun

Ingredients (Serves 2)

- **1 red pepper**
- **250g lean minced turkey**
- **1 rasher smoked streaky bacon, finely chopped**
- **25g onion, finely chopped**
- **40g carrot, peeled and grated**
- **30g dry white breadcrumbs**
- **½tsp salt**
- **1tbsp sweet chilli sauce, plus extra to serve**
- **1tbsp vegetable oil**
- **2 crusty white rolls, split and toasted**
- **Leaves of 1 Little Gem lettuce**
- **2 slices grilled pineapple**

1 Halve and deseed the pepper. Finely chop half and put into a bowl with the turkey, bacon, onion, carrot, breadcrumbs, salt and 1tbsp sweet chilli sauce. Bring the mixture together with your hands and divide into 4 equal portions. Form each into a burger shape about 10cm diameter. Put on a plate lined with baking parchment, cover and chill for 30min or until you are ready to cook.

2 When ready to cook, brush a non-stick frying pan lightly with some of the oil. Heat until hot, add the burgers, reduce the heat to medium and cook for 10min. Brush the tops with oil, turn over and continue to cook for a further 7-8min, until thoroughly cooked.

3 To serve, slice the remaining pepper thinly and place in the rolls along with the lettuce. Pop 2 burgers on top, add pineapple and serve with extra chilli sauce.

Why wait for a barbecue? Serve up this fresh, fruity burger any time

Strawberry And Grape Cheesecake Brûlée

Ingredients (Serves 2)

- **4 digestive biscuits, crushed**
- **2tbsp sweet sherry**
- **100g seedless grapes, halved**
- **80g strawberries, halved**
- **80g low fat soft cheese**
- **80g Greek-style natural yogurt**
- **4tsp demerara sugar**

1 Preheat the grill. Scatter the biscuit crumbs over the base of a grill-proof dish. Sprinkle the sherry over them.

2 Mix together the grapes and strawberries and arrange these over the biscuit crumbs in an even layer.

3 Beat the soft cheese and yogurt together until smooth, then spoon it over the fruit – though there's no need to cover it all. Sprinkle the sugar over the cheese mixture.

4 Grill the dessert to melt and brown the sugar, though watch carefully as you don't want it to burn. Cool for a few minutes, then serve.

RECIPE AND STYLING: SUE ASHWORTH
PHOTOGRAPHY: JONATHAN SHORT

Chocolate Cherry Tarts

For a stunning yet simple finish...

Ingredients (Serves 2)

- **50g dark chocolate, chopped**
- **100g double cream**
- **2 individual sweet pastry cases**
- **Cocoa powder, for sprinkling**
- **A few fresh cherries**

1 Put the chocolate into a heatproof bowl. Reserve 2tbsp cream, then put the rest into a non-stick saucepan and heat gently until almost boiling. Pour it over the chocolate, leave for a few moments, then stir until blended and smooth.

2 When the chocolate mousse has cooled slightly, share it between the pastry tarts. Cool completely.

3 Whip the reserved cream until thick. Spoon on to the tarts, sprinkle with cocoa powder and pop cherries on the top. Serve with extra cherries.

Season Of Mists And Twinkling Fairy Lights

Make Christmas fun and festive with this special selection of dishes

This is one of the most beautiful times of the year. The leaves, once green, change to gold and brown, falling to the ground to provide a magical, soft carpet for us to walk upon. Autumn is like living in a painting. Every scene is beautiful, every sunset memorable.

And now is the time to plan ahead, and make Christmas easy this year. With recipes for gifts, treats and cakes, we have a complete celebration dinner for two, a delicious breakfast to start your day, a selection of tasty bites which will work well as alternative starters, an evening treat or if

> *Christmas is the day that holds all time together – Alexander Smith*

you have invited people round for a festive party. And, of course, a showstopping cake! Jingle jingle!

RECIPE AND STYLING: SUE ASHWORTH
PHOTOGRAPHY: JONATHAN SHORT

STEP BY STEP
Gingerbread House

You won't need planning permission for this sweet seasonal centrepiece!

Ingredients (Makes 1 house)
- **200g dark muscovado sugar**
- **250g butter**
- **7tbsp (150g) golden syrup**
- **650g plain flour, plus extra for sprinkling**
- **5tsp ground ginger**
- **2tsp bicarbonate of soda**
- **Several sheets of baking paper**

Decoration
- **1 egg white**
- **250g icing sugar**
- **250g pack flower and moulding paste (Renshaw Decor-ice)**
- **Selection of small sweets, silver balls, etc.**

1 Put the sugar into a large saucepan. Cut the butter into pieces and add to the pan. Measure in the syrup. If you prefer, put the pan onto digital scales, zero them, and weigh in the syrup to exactly the correct amount. Heat gently to melt slowly, stirring occasionally. Do not allow the mixture to boil.

2 Sift the plain flour, ginger and bicarbonate of soda into a large mixing bowl, stirring to mix thoroughly. Pour in the melted mixture and stir together with a wooden spoon to make a stiff dough, using your hand to bring the mixture together. Preheat the oven to 200°C/fan oven 180°C/Gas Mark 6.

3 Put a sheet of baking paper onto a work surface and sprinkle it with a little flour. Take about a quarter of the dough and press it out with your fingertips until it's quite flat (this is easier than rolling, as it helps prevent it from cracking). Now take a lightly floured rolling pin and carefully roll out until it's about 0.5cm in thickness.

4 Cut out the first shape for your house using a cutter or template. Remove the cutter or template, then slide the section, still on the baking paper, onto a baking sheet. Roll out more dough, re-using trimmings, until you have 2 side walls, 2 roof panels and 2 gable ends. Use trimmings to make a chimney, trees and stars.

5 You will need to bake in batches, each 11-12min, until firm and darker round the edges. Before you cook the front gable end, use cutters or templates to remove the door and mark 2 windows (removed more easily once baked). After baking, cool all sections on the tray for a few minutes before transferring to a wire rack.

6 Roll out the moulding paste on a surface dusted with icing sugar. Cut out 4 window frames. Use a small round or heart-shaped cutter to stamp out about 60 roof slates. Leave to harden for 20min. Beat egg white and icing sugar together to make a thick icing. Place in a piping bag. Use the icing to fix on window frames and roof slates.

7 Pipe icing thickly onto a cake board where each panel will stand. Put the first panel in place. Pipe icing thickly along the wall edge. Fix on the gable end, using a butter dish or bowl for support until 3 pieces are fixed. Remove the support and fix on the front gable end. Leave for 20min, then fix on roof. Leave overnight. Decorate with sweets, fixing in place with icing.

Five Golden Rules

◆ **Be patient. This is not to be rushed!**
◆ **Measure ingredients accurately so that the gingerbread bakes without expanding.**
◆ **Roll and cut out each piece on baking paper, then slide onto baking trays. Trim baked pieces with a sharp knife for straight edges.**
◆ **Get help to construct the house. Ensure the icing "cement" is thick enough; hold walls together for 2-3min to set, before adding the roof.**
◆ **Decorate as you wish!**

Added Extras

Make up a batch of dough with half quantities, then create these wonderfully festive biscuits for hanging from the tree or to fix to the house. Or make Christmas trees that can be used to stand around your gingerbread house!

Tree decorations: Roll out the dough to about the thickness of two £1 coins. Stamp out cookies with a snowflake cutter, and arrange on a baking sheet lined with baking paper. Bake for 8-10min. Cool, then decorate with small sweets, silver balls and edible glitter. Thread some ribbon or raffia around them for hanging on the tree.

Christmas trees: Roll out the dough and use a Christmas tree cutter to stamp out shapes. Bake as above. Decorate with royal icing (as used for the house) and fix small sweets and silver balls onto the icing, with a star-shaped sweet at the top. Stand them up in blobs of white moulding paste or ready-to-roll icing. Scatter a little icing sugar on top to look like snow.

Spiced Nuts

An attractive gift with extra bite!

Ingredients (Makes 550g)

- **2tbsp Worcestershire sauce**
- **1tsp chilli powder**
- **2tbsp olive oil**
- **1tsp sea salt flakes**
- **½tsp paprika**
- **1tsp caster sugar**
- **500g mixed nuts eg cashews, almonds, pecans, walnuts and pistachios**

1. Preheat the oven to 180°C/Fan 160°C/Gas 4. Combine the Worcestershire sauce, chilli powder, olive oil, sea salt, paprika and sugar in a large bowl. Add the nuts and stir together.

2. Spread on to a baking sheet lined with non-stick baking paper and bake for 10 minutes, turning after 5 minutes. Transfer to a tray lined with kitchen paper and leave to cool.

3. Store in an airtight container for up to 3 weeks. If giving as a gift, in cellophane packaging, label with a use-by date of 7 days.

RECIPE AND STYLING: JENNIE SHAPTER
PHOTOGRAPHY: JON WHITAKER

Fruit Curd

Make jars of glowing golden indulgence

Ingredients
(Makes about 575g)

For Lemon and Lime Curd:
- 3 limes
- 2 lemons
- 2 large eggs and
- 2 large egg yolks
- 250g caster sugar
- 100g butter

1 Grate the rind from 1 lime and 2 lemons. Squeeze the juice from the limes and lemons and place in a heatproof bowl with the rinds. Add the eggs, sugar and butter.

2 Place over a pan of simmering water and stir with a wooden spoon until the sugar dissolves. Continue stirring until thick enough to coat the back of the spoon.

3 Pour through a sieve into a clean jug and then into sterilised jars. Cover and store in the fridge.

For Orange Curd:

Use 2tbsp lemon juice, the juice of 3 oranges and the grated rind or 1 orange instead of the limes and lemons. Follow the method above.

The curd can be created up to two weeks in advance and makes a lovely gift for a friend

Dundee Cake

Take the time to create a traditional treat!

Ingredients
(Makes 1 x 20cm cake)

- **175g currants**
- **325g sultanas**
- **125g mixed peel**
- **50g blanched almonds, chopped**
- **Grated zest of 1 large orange**
- **275g plain flour**
- **250g butter, cut into pieces**
- **250g light brown soft sugar**
- **4 eggs**
- **2tbsp Seville orange marmalade**
- **About 65g whole blanched almonds, to decorate**

1 Grease and line a 20cm deep loose-based cake tin. Preheat the oven to 170°C/Fan 150°C/Gas 3. Combine the currants, sultanas, peel, almonds and orange zest in a bowl. Add half the flour and stir together thoroughly.

2 Place the butter and sugar in a large bowl and beat together until light and fluffy. Gradually beat in the eggs. Fold in the remaining flour, then the fruit, nut and flour mixture. Finally stir in the marmalade.

3 Spoon into the prepared tin and make a slight hollow in the centre of the cake with the spoon. Place the whole almonds, in circles, on top of the cake. Bake for 2 hours, or until a skewer inserted in the centre comes out clean. If necessary, cover the top with foil towards the end of cooking.

4 Leave to cool in the tin. Remove, wrap in greaseproof paper and foil, and store in an airtight container. Leave to mature for at least a week. Use within 6 weeks.

The original Dundee cake recipe dates from the 1700s

RECIPE AND STYLING: JENNIE SHAPTER
PHOTOGRAPHY: JON WHITAKER

Eggy Nog Bread

Just how fun and festive is this?

Ingredients (Serves 6)
- **12 x slices sliced fruit loaf**
- **125g raspberry jam**
- **4 medium eggs**
- **4tbsp whipping cream**
- **¼tsp ground nutmeg**
- **1tsp vanilla extract**
- **2tbsp brandy, optional**
- **40g unsalted butter**
- **1tsp icing sugar**

1 Trim away crusts from bread if preferred, then spread with jam and sandwich 2 slices together. Cut each in half.

2 Beat the eggs with the cream, nutmeg, vanilla and the brandy if using. Pour into a shallow dish. Dip each sandwich in egg on both sides.

3 Melt the butter in a large frying pan until bubbling. Gently fry the sandwiches in 2 batches for about 2min on each side until lightly golden. Drain, arrange on warm platter, dust with icing sugar and serve with fruit.

You're Invited To A Sophisticated Christmas Dinner For Two...

 ## Pear, Chicory And Brie Salad

Elegant and indulgent – no ordinary salad!

Ingredients (Serves 2)
- **1 head chicory (red if available), trimmed and finely sliced**
- **50g fennel, finely sliced**
- **4 radish, finely sliced**
- **1 ripe pear, cored and sliced**
- **2tsp lemon juice**
- **80g Brie, sliced**
- **40g pomegranate seeds**
- **Lamb's lettuce or rocket, to garnish**

Dressing
- **2tbsp lemon juice**
- **4tbsp olive oil**
- **1tsp clear honey**
- **½tsp Dijon or wholegrain mustard**
- **Pinch of salt and freshly ground black pepper**

1 Arrange the chicory, fennel and radish on two serving plates. Toss the pear slices in lemon juice and arrange on top with the sliced Brie.

2 Make the dressing by whisking together the lemon juice, olive oil, honey, mustard and seasoning.

3 When ready to serve, drizzle the dressing over the salads and sprinkle the pomegranate seeds over the top. Garnish with lamb's lettuce or rocket and season with a little extra black pepper.

RECIPE AND STYLING: SUE ASHWORTH
PHOTOGRAPHY: JONATHAN SHORT

★ Bacon-Wrapped Turkey With
★ Apricot Stuffing ★

Christmas dinner reinvented for two!

Ingredients (Serves 2)

- **2 turkey steaks (weighing approx 150g each)**
- **30g ready-to-eat dried apricots, very finely chopped**
- **20g Panko or fresh breadcrumbs**
- **2 spring onions, very finely chopped**
- **15g butter, melted**
- **Finely grated zest of ½ lemon**
- **1tbsp finely chopped fresh parsley**
- **Salt and freshly ground black pepper**
- **1 egg yolk (reserve the white for Crispy Stuffing Balls)**
- **4 rashers streaky bacon**
- **Vegetable oil, for greasing**
- **Cranberry sauce, to serve**

1 Carefully beat out the turkey steaks between sheets of cling film, using a rolling pin, so that they are quite thin.

2 Make the stuffing by mixing together the apricots, breadcrumbs, spring onions, melted butter, lemon zest and parsley. Season with salt and pepper, then mix in the egg yolk.

3 Spread the stuffing evenly over the turkey steaks, then roll them up into a cylinder shape. Wrap each one with two rashers of streaky bacon. Grease two pieces of foil with vegetable oil and wrap the turkey parcels separately. Chill for 15min.

4 Preheat the oven to 200°C, Fan Oven 180°C, Gas Mark 6. Put the foil parcels into a roasting tin and cook for 30min. Unwrap, removing the foil. Drain off any juices and pour these into a measuring jug. Return the turkey to the oven for a further 15-20min to brown and cook through.

5 When cooked, cover with a fresh piece of foil and rest for 10min before slicing and serving with cranberry sauce.

Crispy Stuffing Balls

Ingredients

- **Vegetable oil, for greasing**
- **175g sausagemeat (use approx 3 sausages)**
- **1 small apple, grated**
- **1tsp mixed dried herbs**
- **1 egg white (use one left from turkey filling)**
- **50g Panko or dried breadcrumbs**
- **Salt and black pepper**

1. Line a baking sheet with foil and grease it with vegetable oil. Mix the sausagemeat, apple and dried herbs. Season lightly, then roll into 16 small balls (you'll have some left for later).

2. Lightly beat the egg white in a shallow bowl with 2tbsp water. Put breadcrumbs into a separate bowl. Toss the stuffing balls in the egg white, then roll them in breadcrumbs.

3. Bake in the oven for 30-35min until crispy, turning once halfway through. Serve 3 per person with the turkey.

Rosemary Parmentier Potatoes

Ingredients
- ◆ **3tbsp vegetable oil**
- ◆ **700g potatoes, peeled and cut into cubes**
- ◆ **Sprig of rosemary**

1 Preheat the oven to 200°C, Fan Oven 180°C, Gas Mark 6. Pour the vegetable oil into a roasting pan and heat for 3-4min.

2 Tip the potatoes into the oil and toss to coat. Roast for 45min, turning twice, and snipping the rosemary over the top 5min before the end of cooking time.

> " *Pat potatoes dry with kitchen paper before adding to the oil*

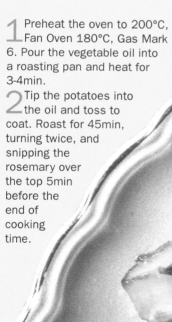

RECIPE AND STYLING: SUE ASHWORTH
PHOTOGRAPHY: JONATHAN SHORT

Christmas Pudding Ice Cream

All the flavours in a lighter dessert!

Ingredients (Serves 2)

- **Preparation time: 20min, plus soaking and freezing**
- **50g ready-to-eat dried apricots, finely chopped**
- **50g glacé cherries, finely chopped**
- **50g raisins or sultanas**
- **2tbsp brandy or rum**
- **500g tub good-quality vanilla ice cream**
- **30g shelled pistachio nuts, finely chopped (optional)**
- **Toffee sauce or golden syrup, for drizzling**
- **Brandy snaps, to serve**

1 A few days before Christmas, prepare the ice cream. Put the apricots, cherries and raisins or sultanas into a bowl and add the brandy or rum. Stir and cover, then leave to soak for several hours, or overnight.

2 Allow the ice cream to soften a little. Scoop it into a bowl and use a fork to break it down, then stir in the soaked fruits and chopped nuts (if using). Tip into a freezer container, level the surface and re-freeze until Christmas Day.

3 To serve, let the ice cream soften for a few minutes so that it is easier to scoop. While doing so, chill two small serving bowls in the freezer. Scoop the ice cream into the bowls and drizzle with toffee sauce or golden syrup. Serve immediately, with some crumbled brandy snap on top and a brandy snap on the side.

Roasted Pepper And Goats' Cheese Croûtes

Tiny titbits of festive indulgence

Ingredients (Serves 2)

- **Vegetable oil**
- **4 slices bread, about 1cm thick**
- **80g butter, melted**
- **50g rocket**
- **150g roasted red peppers from a jar**
- **100g goats' cheese, sliced**
- **4tbsp balsamic glaze**
- **Freshly-ground black pepper**
- **Basil and parsley, to garnish**

1 Preheat the oven to 190°C, Fan Oven 170°C, Gas Mark 5. Grease a baking sheet with a little vegetable oil.

2 Use a 9-10cm cutter to stamp out 4 rounds from the slices of bread. Brush these generously on both sides with melted butter. Place on the baking sheet and bake for 8-10min until golden brown.

3 Arrange the baked bread on 4 serving plates and top with rocket and sliced peppers. Sit a slice of goats' cheese on top, then drizzle with the balsamic glaze. Serve, sprinkled with black pepper and garnished with basil and parsley.

RECIPE AND STYLING: SUE ASHWORTH
PHOTOGRAPHY: JONATHAN SHORT

Prawn And Smoked Salmon Pâté

Add a touch of class to your dinner party

Ingredients (Serves 2)

- **150g low-fat soft cheese**
- **100g crème fraîche**
- **80g smoked salmon, chopped**
- **150g cooked, peeled prawns**
- **1tbsp chopped fresh dill, plus sprigs, to garnish**
- **Freshly-ground black pepper**
- **8 thin slices ciabatta bread**

1 Mix together the soft cheese and crème fraîche, then stir in the smoked salmon.

2 Reserve a few prawns for garnish, then chop the rest and add these to the mixture with the dill. Season with black pepper and mix together. Spoon into 4 small pots, then cover and chill until ready to serve.

3 Garnish with the reserved prawns and dill sprigs, then serve with toasted ciabatta.

The pâté can be served hot or cold, but develops its best flavours after a few days of chilling

Trio Of Tiny Tartlets

Three appetisers to make your mouth melt

Ingredients (Serves 2)

- **12 small savoury pastry cases**
- **3tbsp crème fraîche or soft cheese**
- **80g hot smoked salmon, flaked**
- **Lemon slices, capers and dill, to garnish**
- **½ small avocado, mashed**
- **Cherry tomato quarters and basil, to garnish**
- **2tbsp soured cream**
- **2tbsp grated beetroot (vacuum packed, not in vinegar)**
- **Sliced radish, gherkins and parsley sprigs, to garnish**

1 Put 3 pastry cases onto each of 4 serving plates. Put a heaped tsp of crème fraîche or soft cheese into 4 tartlets, and top with flakes of salmon. Garnish with lemon, capers and dill.

2 Mix the remaining crème fraîche or soft cheese with the avocado and spoon this into 4 more tartlets. Garnish with cherry tomato and basil.

3 Mix most of the soured cream with the beetroot. Spoon this into the remaining 4 tartlets. Top with the remaining soured cream, then garnish with radish, gherkins and parsley sprigs.

RECIPE AND STYLING: SUE ASHWORTH
PHOTOGRAPHY: JONATHAN SHORT

RECIPE AND STYLING: SUE ASHWORTH
PHOTOGRAPHY: JONATHAN SHORT

Rum Mincemeat and Mince Pies

Get ahead for Christmas with these treats

Ingredients
Makes: 3 x 450g jars
mincemeat; 24 mince pies

- **225g seedless raisins**
- **225g currants**
- **225g sultanas**
- **100g glacé cherries, quartered**
- **120ml rum**
- **2tbsp lemon juice**
- **½tsp ground cinnamon**
- **½tsp ground nutmeg**
- **75g butter**
- **175g light muscovado sugar**

For the mince pies:

- **400g plain flour**
- **¼tsp salt**
- **100g chilled butter, cut into pieces**
- **100g white vegetable fat, cut into pieces**
- **2tsp caster sugar**
- **1 egg yolk**
- **Chilled water, to mix**
- **Beaten egg or milk, to glaze**

1 To make the mincemeat, put the dried fruit and cherries in a large mixing bowl with the rum. Stir well, then cover and leave to soak overnight.

2 Next day, stir in the lemon juice, cinnamon and nutmeg. Melt the butter and add the sugar. Heat gently until the sugar dissolves, then stir into the fruit mixture. Pot in sterilised jars. Keep in a cool place for up to 3 months.

3 For the mince pies, sift the flour and salt into a large bowl. Rub in the butter and white vegetable fat until the mixture looks like breadcrumbs. Stir in the sugar and egg yolk, then add just enough chilled water (about 4tbsp) to make a soft (not sticky) dough. Wrap and chill for 15min. Meanwhile, preheat the oven to 200°C, fan oven 180°C, Gas Mark 6.

4 Roll out the pastry on a lightly floured surface and use half to line 2 bun trays. Roll out and cut lids from remaining pastry – in star shapes, if wished.

5 Fill each pastry case with 1tsp mincemeat. Top with the lids, dampened with a little water, and press to seal. Glaze with beaten egg or milk and bake for approx. 20min. Cool, then pack in airtight containers, or freeze in boxes.

Naked Whisky Mac Gateau

A grown-up, contemporary showstopper

Ingredients

- **300g plain flour**
- **10g bicarbonate of soda**
- **4tsp ground ginger**
- **2tsp ground mixed spice**
- **300g soft light brown sugar**
- **3 medium size eggs, beaten**
- **300ml buttermilk**
- **175g unsalted butter, very soft**
- **3 small oranges**
- **300ml double cream**
- **5tbsp whisky**
- **2tbsp clear honey**
- **Frosted rosemary sprigs and orange wedges, to decorate**

1 Preheat oven to 180°C/ Fan Oven 160°C/ Gas Mark 4. Grease and line 3 x 18cm sandwich cake tins. Sift the flour, bicarbonate of soda and spices into a bowl and stir in the brown sugar. Make a well in the centre.

2 Add eggs, buttermilk and butter and mix well to a smooth, thick batter. Divide between the tins, smooth the tops and bake for 30-35min until golden and firm to the touch. Cool for 5min then turn on to a wire rack to cool completely.

3 To decorate, grate the rind from one of the oranges and set aside. Slice off the tops and bottoms from all the oranges and peel away the rind and pith keeping the oranges whole, then slice them thinly.

4 Whip the cream until just peaking and then whisk in the orange rind, 2tbsp whisky and honey. Prick the cakes with a cocktail stick and sprinkle with the remaining whisky, then spread 2 of the cakes with whipped cream. Drain the orange slices and arrange over the top of the cream.

5 Stack the cakes on top of each other and transfer to a plate. Very thinly spread some of the remaining cream round the edge of the cake using a palette knife – you should still be able to see the cake layers. Carefully spread the rest of the cream on top, decorate with the frosted rosemary and orange wedges, and serve.

RECIPE AND STYLING: KATHRYN HAWKINS
PHOTOGRAPHY: STUART MACGREGOR

Cold Outside But Our Hearts Are Warm

Leave winter at the door as you embrace the great indoors for cosy comfort

Winter's cold embrace is upon us. The twinkling frost, with the air fresh and freezing has much to appeal. We love to put on our hats and gloves and venture out for invigorating walks, noses tinged red and fingers often tinged blue!

We silently pray for a blanket of soft, white snow, which may or may not appear, but really, this is the time of year when all we want to do is get cosy.

Hearty dishes, full of flavour and comfort is exactly what we need to ward off the teeth-chattering temperatures. This is food that is placed in bowls to wrap your hands around. Food

> # Winter is the time for comfort, good food and warmth
> ## - Edith Sitwell

that is good for the soul. Sit back, relax and enjoy the comforts of home as the storms rage outside.

STEP BY STEP

Risotto

Love this classic
Italian rice dish?
Then follow our
easy guide
to create a creamy,
delicious plateful!

Ingredients (Serves 4)

- ◆ **2 vegetable stock cubes**
- ◆ **1 bay leaf**
- ◆ **25g butter**
- ◆ **1tbsp olive oil**
- ◆ **300g risotto rice (Arborio or carnaroli)**
- ◆ **200ml dry white wine**
- ◆ **1 bunch spring onions, chopped**
- ◆ **300g butternut squash (weighed when peeled and deseeded), chopped**
- ◆ **75g fine asparagus or green beans, trimmed and chopped**
- ◆ **75g Parmesan cheese**
- ◆ **Salt and freshly ground black pepper**
- ◆ **Basil leaves and Parmesan cheese shavings, to garnish**

1 Prepare the stock. Pour 1.2 litres boiling water into a saucepan. Crumble in the stock cubes. Add the bay leaf and simmer for 10min. You could make up part of the stock with reserved cooking water from carrots or leeks, and add a few parsley sprigs. This quantity gives plenty of stock – you may not need it all.

2 In a very large, deep frying pan, heat the butter and olive oil together. Remember, the pan needs to be large, as the rice expands to almost fill it! Add the rice and sauté it gently over a low heat, stirring often, until it looks translucent. This will take about 3-4min. Keep an eye on the rice and don't leave it unattended, as it must not brown.

3 Pour the white wine into the rice, tipping it in all at once. Let it bubble up, then allow it to settle down and cook gently until all the wine has been absorbed. Stir the rice frequently to make sure that it doesn't start to catch on the bottom of the pan. You'll find that it will take 3-4min cooking on a low heat for the liquid to be absorbed.

4 Before you add the butternut squash to the frying pan, check that the cubes are small enough – they should be no more than (roughly!) 1cm, as they need to cook with the rice until tender. Add them to the frying pan with the spring onions, stirring them in. Cook over a low heat, stirring, for 2min. Don't allow the rice or vegetables to brown.

5 Ladle about ¼ of the hot stock into the rice, stir it in, then allow to simmer gently until it has been absorbed. It's really important to cook the rice slowly, so that it gradually becomes tender all the way through. Don't stir all the time – it's not necessary, and can break down the rice grains too much to give a stodgy texture.

6 Keep ladling in hot stock as soon as the last ladleful has been absorbed. From the time you start adding it, the rice will cook in 20-25min. Add the asparagus after cooking the rice for 12-15min – it needs about 8-10min. It's good if the asparagus retains a little "bite", though add it earlier if the stalks are thick, or chop them smaller.

7 Taste the rice from time to time to check when it's tender. As soon as it is, grate in the Parmesan cheese finely and stir it through gently. Remember to always stir the risotto gently, not vigorously – it's one of the secrets to its success. Share the risotto between 4 warm plates and serve topped with basil leaves and Parmesan shavings.

Five Golden Rules

- ◆ The right variety of rice is essential.
- ◆ Stir often, gently. Add liquid gradually and simmer slowly. Patience, please!
- ◆ Choose a wine you'd be happy to drink, and stock cubes with a good flavour. Knorr are good, and Marigold bouillon powder works well too.
- ◆ Buy a piece of Parmesan and grate it yourself. It will have a better flavour.
- ◆ Be ready to eat when the risotto is done – if it's left waiting, it will end up going stodgy.

Added Extras

Chicken, Chorizo & Pepper Risotto
Use a large chopped, deseeded red pepper instead of squash and chicken stock instead of vegetable. At the same time, add 100g sliced chorizo. When almost ready add 200g chopped cooked chicken and a few halved cherry tomatoes. Cook until the rice is tender and the chicken is heated through.

Arancini – Risotto Balls
This is the most fabulous way to use up leftover risotto! Simply add 1 beaten egg to a half quantity of risotto, then form into egg-sized ovals. Dip in beaten egg, then roll in breadcrumbs to coat (panko breadcrumbs work well). Deep fry or shallow fry until golden brown and serve with a little grated Parmesan.

RECIPE AND STYLING: MAXINE CLARK
PHOTOGRAPHY: LIGHTHOUSE

Curried Parsnip And Apple Soup

Aromatic, sweet and deliciously warming

Ingredients (Serves 6)

- **40g butter**
- **1tbsp vegetable oil**
- **2 medium onions, chopped**
- **2 garlic cloves, chopped**
- **1 medium cooking apple, peeled, cored and chopped**
- **1-2tbsp medium curry powder**
- **1tsp turmeric**
- **1tsp ground ginger**
- **700g parsnips, roughly chopped**
- **1.2 litres vegetable or chicken stock**
- **Salt and freshly-ground black pepper**

1 Heat the butter and oil in a large saucepan until the butter begins to foam, then add the onions, garlic and apple and cook gently for about 5min. Stir in the curry powder, turmeric and ginger, stir and cook gently for 5min more.

2 Add the parsnips, stir well, then pour in the stock. Season, then bring to the boil, turn down the heat and simmer uncovered very gently for 45min.

3 Remove from the heat, then liquidise with a stick blender or in a liquidiser. Return to the saucepan, taste and adjust the seasoning. Reheat immediately, or when required. Garnish with toasted mixed seeds and serve with seeded rolls or cheese scones.

A great, tasty way to use up cheap, plentiful parsnips

Roasted Tomato And Red Pepper Soup

Velvety smooth with a strong flavour kick

Ingredients (Serves 6)

- **900g ripe plum tomatoes (or 3 cans whole plum tomatoes)**
- **8 medium red peppers, halved and seeded**
- **1-2 fresh red chillies (optional), seeded**
- **3 large garlic cloves, peeled**
- **6tbsp olive oil**
- **2-3tsp smoked sweet paprika (pimentón)**
- **1.2 litres vegetable or chicken stock**
- **Sea salt and freshly-ground black pepper**

1 Preheat oven to 220°C, Fan Oven 200°C, Gas 7.

2 Pull stalks off the fresh tomatoes and halve them. If using canned tomatoes open then tip them into a sieve placed over a bowl to catch the juice (reserve it).

3 Put tomatoes, peppers, chillies and garlic cloves into a large roasting tin (or two so the vegetables aren't too cramped) and toss them in the olive oil. Season well and roast in the oven for about 20min until all the vegetables are soft and slightly charred at the edges.

4 Tip half the vegetables into a liquidiser, pour in half the stock, the reserved tomato juice and the paprika and liquidise until smooth. Pour into a saucepan and repeat with all remaining vegetables and stock. Reheat until almost boiling, taste and season. Serve with chunky croutons and savoury scones.

RECIPE AND STYLING: MAXINE CLARK
PHOTOGRAPHY: LIGHTHOUSE

Croque Monsieur

The original French fast food from 1910

Ingredients (Serves 1)
- ◆ **2 thick slices of bread or brioche**
- ◆ **2 thick slices Gruyère, Gouda or Emmental**
- ◆ **1 thin slice ham**
- ◆ **1tsp butter**

1 Heat a toasted sandwich maker or grill and butter the bread. Put a slice of cheese on each slice of bread. Sandwich the ham between the slices.

2 Heat the sandwich maker and transfer the sandwich to cook for about 5min. Alternatively grill or fry, turning once.

Spread on 1tsp Dijon mustard for an authentic French flavour

Chicken Roasted With Indian Spices

A roast to make your taste buds sing!

Ingredients
(Serves 2, with leftovers!)

- **1 medium chicken**
- **2tbsp vegetable oil**
- **1tsp ground turmeric**
- **1tsp ground coriander**
- **1tsp cumin seeds**
- **2 limes, sliced**
- **1 red or green chilli, deseeded and sliced**
- **1 large garlic clove, thinly sliced**
- **Salt and freshly ground black pepper**
- **Fresh coriander sprigs, to serve**

1 Preheat the oven to 200°C, fan oven 180°C, Gas Mark 6. Put the chicken into a roasting tin.

2 Mix together the oil, turmeric, coriander and cumin seeds. Rub all over the chicken. Season with salt and black pepper.

3 Cover the bird with foil and roast for between 1½hrs and 1hr 40min. Around 20min before the end of the cooking time remove the foil and add the lime wedges, chilli and garlic.

4 Check that the chicken is fully cooked by inserting a sharp knife into the thickest part. There should be no trace of pink juices. If necessary, cook a little longer.

5 Cover the chicken with foil and allow it to rest for 10min before carving. Garnish with fresh coriander and serve with turmeric potatoes (see next page).

RECIPE AND STYLING: SUE ASHWORTH
PHOTOGRAPHY: JONATHAN SHORT

RECIPE AND STYLING: SUE ASHWORTH
PHOTOGRAPHY: JONATHAN SHORT

Roasted Turmeric Potatoes With Chicken And Peppers

Perfect to accompany your spicy roast

Ingredients (Serves 2)

- **400g small new potatoes**
- **2tbsp vegetable oil**
- **1tsp ground turmeric**
- **½tsp cumin seeds (optional)**
- **3 small red or yellow peppers, halved and deseeded**
- **1 small red onion, sliced into thin wedges**
- **2 cooked chicken legs (from the main roast)**
- **Handful of young spinach leaves**
- **Salt and freshly ground black pepper**

For the cucumber raita:

- **¼ cucumber, finely chopped**
- **100g plain yogurt**
- **Pinch of salt**

1 Preheat the oven to 200°C, fan oven 180°C, Gas Mark 6.

2 Put the potatoes into a roasting tin with the vegetable oil and turmeric, tossing to coat. Season. Roast for 30min, then add the cumin seeds (if using), peppers and onion and roast for a further 20min, until tender.

3 Meanwhile, make the raita by mixing together the cucumber and yogurt with a pinch of salt. Keep chilled.

4 Serve the potatoes with chicken legs from the main roast, sprinkled with the spinach leaves. Serve the cucumber raita on the side.

A spoonful of mango chutney will add fruity freshness

Chicken Naan With Kachumber

Ingredients (Serves 2)

- 2 tomatoes, finely chopped
- ¼ cucumber, finely chopped
- 2 spring onions, finely chopped
- 1 fresh green chilli, deseeded and very finely chopped
- 2tbsp chopped fresh coriander, plus sprigs to garnish
- Few drops of olive or vegetable oil
- 2 mini naan breads
- 100g roast chicken, torn into pieces

1 Make the kachumber by mixing together the tomatoes, cucumber, spring onions, chilli and coriander. Add a few drops of oil and season with salt and pepper.

2 Warm the naan breads in a toaster or under the grill.

3 Pile the kachumber and roast chicken on top of the naan breads. Serve with a spoonful of raita (see turmeric potato recipe on previous page for details).

RECIPE AND STYLING: SUE ASHWORTH
PHOTOGRAPHY: JONATHAN SHORT

Sausage And Lentil Bake

Simple to make, but so rich and satisfying

Ingredients (Serves 2)

- **6 pork sausages (or use vegetarian sausages)**
- **A little vegetable oil**
- **1 garlic clove, crushed**
- **1 red onion, sliced**
- **1 red pepper, deseeded and chopped**
- **1 carrot, thinly sliced**
- **400g can chopped tomatoes**
- **400g can green lentils, rinsed and drained**
- **1tsp dried mixed herbs**
- **1 chicken or vegetable stock cube**
- **Salt and freshly-ground black pepper**
- **Parsley sprigs, to garnish**

1 Preheat the oven to 180°C, Fan Oven 160°C, Gas Mark 4. Put the sausages into a baking dish, brush with a little vegetable oil, then bake for 15-20min until browned.

2 Add the garlic, onion, red pepper, carrot, tomatoes, lentils and herbs. Dissolve the stock cube in 300ml boiling water and add to the dish, stirring gently to mix it in. Season.

3 Cover the dish tightly with foil and bake for 1hr 15min. Serve, garnished with parsley.

Lentils add iron, heart-healthy polyphenols and bags of protein. They're great in salads too

Winter Vegetable Turkey Stir-Fry

A whole new twist on a festive favourite

Ingredients (Serves 2)

- **1tbsp vegetable oil**
- **250g turkey breast chunks or stir-fry strips**
- **1 carrot, finely sliced**
- **1 small red onion, finely sliced**
- **2 celery sticks, finely sliced**
- **80g small sprouts, trimmed and halved**
- **50g Savoy or white cabbage, shredded**
- **5cm piece root ginger, peeled and thinly sliced**
- **1 garlic clove, thinly sliced**
- **2tbsp soy sauce**
- **Freshly-ground black pepper**
- **Sweet chilli sauce, for drizzling**
- **Fresh chives, to garnish**

1 Heat the vegetable oil in a wok or large frying pan and stir-fry the turkey over a high heat for 3-4min, until browned.

2 Add the carrot, onion, celery and sprouts and stir-fry for 3-4min. Add the cabbage, ginger and garlic and stir-fry for another 2-3min. Season with the soy sauce and black pepper.

3 Serve, sprinkled with sweet chilli sauce and fresh chives.

RECIPE AND STYLING: SUE ASHWORTH
PHOTOGRAPHY: JONATHAN SHORT

RECIPE AND STYLING: SUE ASHWORTH
PHOTOGRAPHY: JONATHAN SHORT

Potato, Onion And Bacon Hotpot

Four main ingredients, and oh so comforting

Ingredients (Serves 2)

- ◆ **800g potatoes, peeled and thinly sliced**
- ◆ **2 medium onions, thinly sliced**
- ◆ **1litre chicken or vegetable stock (2 cubes)**
- ◆ **Freshly-ground black pepper**
- ◆ **4 rashers thick-cut back bacon**
- ◆ **Tomato ketchup, to serve**

1 Preheat the oven to 190°C, Fan Oven 170°C, Gas Mark 5.

2 Arrange the potato and onion slices in alternate layers in a baking dish or casserole dish, seasoning with pepper, and finishing with a layer of potatoes.

3 Pour in the stock. Transfer to the oven and bake for 1¼hr, arranging the bacon rashers on the top for the final 15min. The potatoes should be tender, and the top layer of potatoes and the bacon should be crispy. If necessary, finish off for 5min under the grill.

4 Serve with some tomato ketchup.

For an all-day breakfast feel, serve with halved beef tomatoes and Portobello mushrooms, grilled

Prawn And Mussel Chowder

Simple seafood

Ingredients (Serves 2)

- **1 medium potato, peeled and cut into dice**
- **700ml vegetable stock**
- **4 spring onions, trimmed and chopped**
- **80g frozen peas**
- **80g frozen sweetcorn**
- **100g frozen prawns**
- **1 x 250g pouch mussels in white wine sauce**
- **Freshly-ground black pepper**
- **Parsley sprigs, to garnish**

1. Put the potato into a large saucepan with the stock and spring onions. Simmer gently for 8-10min until just tender.

2. Add the peas, sweetcorn, prawns and mussels, along with the white wine sauce. Simmer gently for 5min, until piping hot.

3. Serve, seasoned with black pepper and garnished with parsley sprigs. Good with warm crusty bread to mop up those delicious juices!

RECIPE AND STYLING: SUE ASHWORTH
PHOTOGRAPHY: JONATHAN SHORT

RECIPE AND STYLING: SUE ASHWORTH
PHOTOGRAPHY: JONATHAN SHORT

Chicken Ramen

Cook up an authentic taste of Asia...

Ingredients (Serves 2)

- **1 sachet miso stock paste (or use 1 chicken stock cube and 1tbsp soy sauce)**
- **150g medium egg noodles**
- **6 spring onions, trimmed and sliced**
- **A few slices of fresh red chilli**
- **100g closed cup mushrooms, sliced**
- **200g skinless roast chicken breast, torn into pieces**
- **1 head pak choi, stems shredded**
- **Fresh chives, to garnish**

1 Put the miso paste (or stock cube and soy sauce) into a wok and add 500ml boiling water. Stir well.

2 Add the noodles and spring onions to the wok and cook over a medium heat for 5min. Stir in the chilli slices, mushrooms, chicken and pak choi stems and leaves. Cook gently for a further 5min until piping hot.

3 Check the seasoning, and then serve, garnished with fresh chives.

Rhubarb Crumble

A sweet and sour dish for those cold nights

Ingredients
- **500g rhubarb, cut into 2.5cm lengths**
- **75g caster sugar**
- **1tsp cornflour**
- **For the topping:**
- **75g plain flour**
- **25g polenta**
- **1tsp ground ginger**
- **50g low fat spread**
- **50g jumbo porridge oats**
- **50g light brown sugar**

1 Place the rhubarb and caster sugar in a saucepan and add 1tbsp water. Cover and simmer on a low heat, until just softened. Stir in the cornflour and transfer to a 20cm pie dish.

2 Preheat the oven to 190°C/Fan170°C/Gas 5. In a large bowl mix together the flour, polenta and ginger. Rub the low-fat spread into the mix until it resembles fine breadcrumbs. Stir in the oats and sugar. Scatter over the rhubarb.

3 Bake for 25-30min, until the crumble is golden. Leave to stand for 5min before serving.

You can enjoy this warming dessert with a clear conscience – it contains just 325 calories per serving

RECIPE AND STYLING: SUE ASHWORTH
PHOTOGRAPHY: JONATHAN SHORT

Winter Berry Free-Form Pie

Is it a pie… or a scrumptious parcel?

Ingredients

- **225g plain flour**
- **½tsp salt**
- **110g butter, chilled and cut into pieces**
- **1 egg, beaten**
- **Chilled water, to mix**
- **50g ground almonds**
- **225g strawberries, halved**
- **200g raspberries**
- **100g blueberries**
- **75g caster sugar, plus extra for sprinkling**

Cooked flat on a baking sheet, with no sticking to the pie dish

1. Preheat the oven to 200°C, fan 180°C, Gas 6.

2. Sift the flour and salt into a large bowl. Rub in butter until the mixture looks like fine crumbs. Stir in 2tbsp beaten egg and just enough chilled water to make a soft, not sticky, dough. Knead lightly until smooth. Wrap and chill for 10min.

3. Roll out the pastry on a lightly floured surface into a circle with a diameter of about 38cm. Transfer to a baking sheet (the pastry will overlap the sheet). Brush the surface with beaten egg.

4. Sprinkle the ground almonds over the pastry to within 7cm of the edge, then scatter the strawberries, raspberries, blueberries and sugar on top. Fold the pastry border over the fruit, tucking and sealing it to make a free-form pie. Brush with beaten egg and sprinkle with sugar.

5. Bake for 25-30min, until pastry is crisp and golden. Serve warm or cold with ice cream, cream or custard.

INDEX

135

Notes: Spring

Notes: Summer

Notes: Christmas

Notes: Cosy

PACKED WITH GREAT READING!

Valentine's Day Best Buys

Feb 9 – Feb 16, 2021
No 5561

LOVE

My Weekly

Your Feel Good Read

www.myweekly.co.uk

£1.50

FOOD THAT WE LOVE!

8 Classic Recipes

4 Romantic Stories

Covid Vaccine

Dr Sarah Has All The Facts

Linda Robson

"I Never Have Regrets!"

Competition open to UK and Republic of Ireland residents only, unless otherwise stated.

"Farming gives us freedom"

The Yorkshire Shepherdess

Pyjama Party!

Cosy Fashion

Inspiring Real Life

"Cancer changed me as a doctor"

Don't Miss

My Weekly

On Sale Every Tuesday

It's Your Feel Good Read!

◆ Spectacular Cookery
◆ Compelling Fiction
◆ Fabulous Fashion And Beauty
◆ Stunning Homes And Gardens
◆ Celebrities You Love
◆ All The Latest Health And Wellbeing News